INSPIRATION UNPLUGGED

Faithful Fridays

A COLLECTION OF FAITHFUL FRIDAY INSPIRATIONAL QUOTES

TERRI AVERY

© Copyright 2015

Faithful Fridays

A COLLECTION OF FAITHFUL FRIDAY INSPIRATIONAL QUOTES

© Copyright 2015
Inspiration Unplugged
Terri Avery
Photographs by Terri Avery

International Standard Book Number
978-0692594773

Acknowledgments

I want to thank my husband Chris Clay
for the inspiration of this book.
We've been to many beautiful places on the
planet together, but the most beautiful
place has been you, in my heart.

I Love You.

Forward

It's very unusual that 2 of your spiritual leaders pass away in the same weekend.

That's what happened to me the weekend of August 29 & 30, 2015.

The Bishop and senior pastor of Nations Ford Community Church, Dr. Phillip M. Davis died of an accidental gun shot wound on Saturday, August 29th. One day shy of his 63rd birthday.

He was not only the Pastor of the church, but a friend. His sermons helped inspire many of the words in this book.

On August 30, 2015, Dr. Wayne Dyer, motivational speaker and author, died of an apparent heart attack at his home on Maui, Hawaii. His books and lectures inspired my way of thinking about my purpose and how to live it for years.

I will miss these two spiritual leaders, but I also know that I am connected to them even in death, for they've made a mark on the world and in me.

Faithful Fridays

FAITH IS THE OPPOSITE OF FEAR.
IF YOU HAVE FEAR, YOUR FAITH CANNOT
BE ACTIVATED.
REPLACE FEAR WITH FAITH AND WATCH
GOD MOVE IN YOUR LIFE

WHEN YOU LIVE BY FAITH,
GOD NEVER FAILS TO ACT.

❧⤳ ·· ⤲❧

WE DON'T HAVE TO KNOW THE FUTURE
TO HAVE FAITH IN GOD;
WE JUST HAVE TO HAVE FAITH IN GOD
TO BE SECURE ABOUT THE FUTURE.

Faithful Fridays

WHEN YOU'RE PRAYING FOR
SUPERNATURAL BLESSINGS,
HAVE FAITH IN GOD.

STAY FAITHFUL IN YOUR WALK WITH GOD
AND HE PROMISES TO GIVE YOU
THE DESIRES OF YOUR HEART.

WHEN YOU NEED A SUPERNATURAL
MOVEMENT IN YOUR LIFE,
RELEASE THE POWER WITHIN,
THE POWER OF FAITH

Faithful Fridays

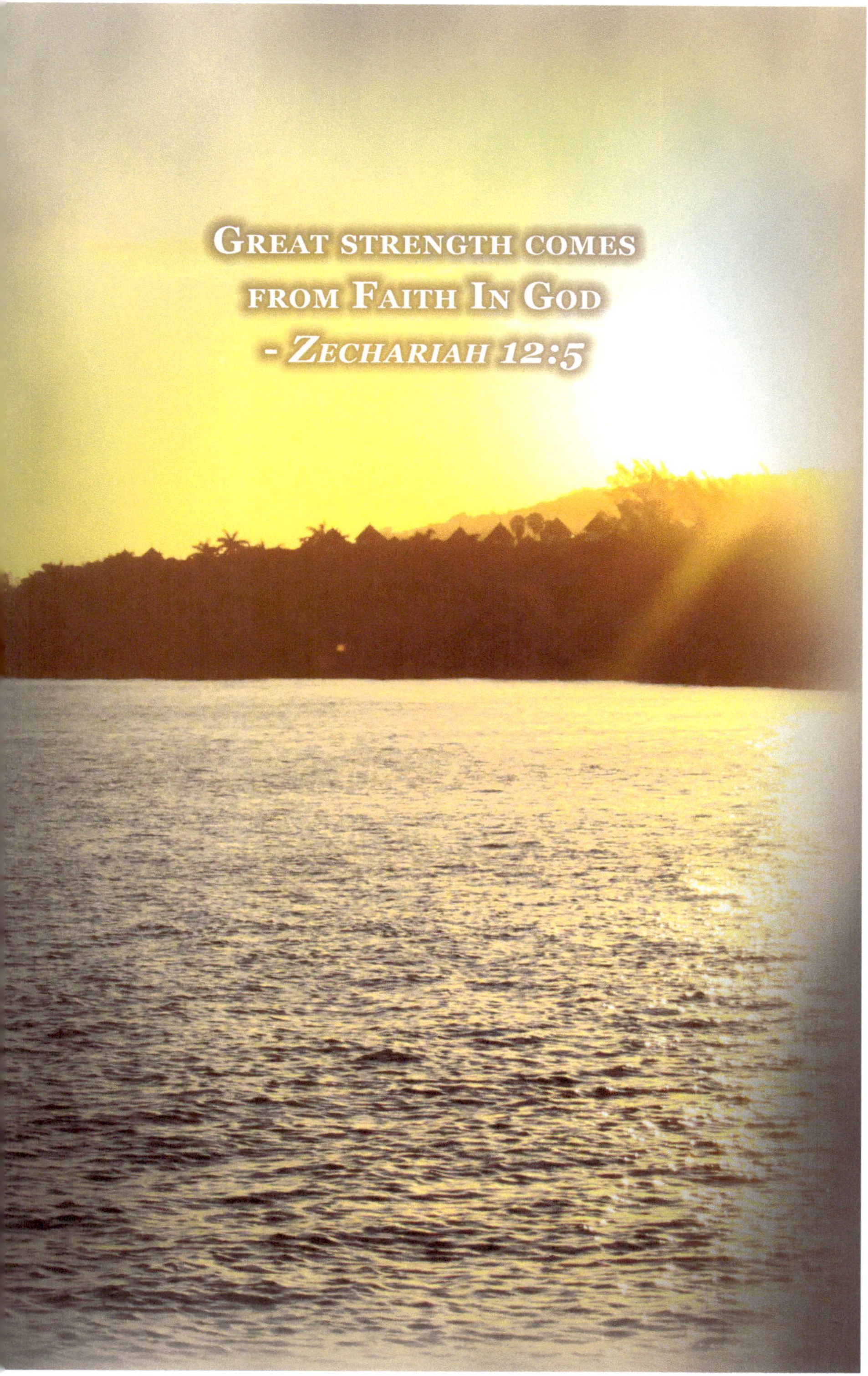
GREAT STRENGTH COMES
FROM FAITH IN GOD
- ZECHARIAH 12:5

THE LORD REWARDS EVERYONE FOR HIS
RIGHTEOUSNESS AND HIS FAITHFULNESS
- *1 SAMUEL 26:23*

FAITH IN GOD HAS SUSTAINED ME

❦

FAITH IS NOT BELIEVING GOD MIGHT,
IT'S KNOWING HE HAS!

Faithful Fridays

FAITH MUST BE A LIFESTYLE!

FAITH IS BELIEVING THAT YOU HAVE
RECEIVED, WALK BY FAITH NOT BY SIGHT.

⤳ .. ⤝

WHEN LIFE IS FILLED WITH UPS AND
DOWNS, STAY FAITHFUL...
GOD WILL GET YOU THROUGH.
WHEN YOU'RE ON AN UP, HOLD ON TO
THAT FAITH, KEEP GOD FIRST,
SO THAT THE DOWNS DON'T SEEM AS BAD.

Faithful Fridays

WHAT ARE YOU BELIEVING GOD FOR?
STAY IN A FAITH FILLED CONSCIOUSNESS
TO GET DREAMS FULFILLED.

HAVING FAITH MEANS NEVER WORRYING
ABOUT WHEN YOUR BLESSINGS WILL COME.
HAVING FAITH IS KNOWING YOU
HAVE ALREADY RECEIVED IT.

⤙⤚

WHEN YOU ARE WAITING FOR SUPERNATURAL
BLESSINGS STAY FAITHFUL TO GOD.
HE IS GOING TO MOVE IN YOUR LIFE.
THE MORE YOU FEEL OVERWHELMED BY
THE DREAM KILLERS, THE CLOSER YOU ARE
TO YOUR BLESSING.

Faithful Fridays

WHEN YOU HAVE FAITH FILLED PRAYERS,
GOD WILL SHOW UP WITH THE
ANSWER HE KNOWS YOU NEED.

SOMETIMES WE WANT TO QUESTION
HOW GOD ANSWERS A PRAYER.
KNOW THAT HE HAS PLANS TO
PROSPER YOU AND NOT HARM YOU.
JUST BELIEVE AND HAVE FAITH.

≫·•·≪

FAITH THAT'S NOT TESTED CANNOT
BE TRUSTED. YOU CAN'T GET THE
BLESSING WITHOUT THE TESTING.

Faithful Fridays

KEEP YOUR MIND ON THOUGHTS OF GOD.
STAY FAITHFUL TO HIS WORD AND
YOU WILL SEE MIRACLES HAPPEN
IN YOUR LIFE.

GOD WILL MAKE THE TRANSITION,
I ONLY HAVE TO BELIEVE AND HAVE FAITH.

FAITH IS TRUSTING GOD.
TURN ON YOUR FAITH WITH DESIRE,
VISION AND DEDICATION AND WATCH
GOD WORK MIRACLES IN YOUR LIFE!

Faithful Fridays

FAITH IS NOT WISHING SOMETHING GOOD
WILL HAPPEN,
FAITH IS KNOWING SOMETHING GOOD
HAS ALREADY HAPPENED.

GROW YOUR FAITH BY READING THE WORD
OF GOD EVERYDAY, PRAYING IN SPIRIT,
INCREASING YOUR FORGIVENESS,
AND LOVING UNCONDITIONALLY.

⋙ ·· ⋘

WALKING BY FAITH AND NOT BY SIGHT
ANTICIPATES THAT YOUR PRAYER HAS
ALREADY BEEN ANSWERED.

Faithful Fridays

FAITH IS A SUPERNATURAL POWER
THAT ONCE YOU BELIEVE
WITHOUT SEEING,
EVERYTHING IS POSSIBLE

DON'T WAIVER, STAY STRONG IN FAITH.

⌁⌁⌁

HAVE FAITH IN THE GRACE OF GOD TO
SUSTAIN YOU THROUGH HARD TIMES.

Faithful Fridays

OUTRAGEOUS FAITH never tires of waiting on the LORD

FAITH IN GOD SHOUTS VICTORY,
BEFORE THE VICTORY

❧ · · ❧

TAKE A LEAP OF FAITH.
GET OUT OF YOUR COMFORT ZONE
TO ACT ON A DREAM.

Faithful Fridays

SOMETIMES WE ARE TEMPTED TO TAKE
SHORT CUTS AND HELP GOD OUT.
GOD DOESN'T NEED OUR HELP
JUST YOUR FAITH.

GOD ALLOWS DIFFICULTY, PROBLEMS AND
CHALLENGES TO COME IN YOUR LIFE.
YOU GOT TO KEEP BELIEVING WHEN
NOTHING IS HAPPENING, THAT'S FAITH

⮞⋯⮜

FAITH IS TOTAL DEPENDENCE ON GOD.
IF YOU DON'T ACT IN FAITH,
YOU DON'T BELIEVE IN GOD.

Faithful Fridays

WHATEVER YOUR TRIAL MAY BE, KNOW
THAT GOD HAS PURPOSE IN ADVERSITY,
AND HE HAS ALLOWED IT.
CONTINUE TO HAVE FAITH IN GOD
TO BRING YOU OUT.

WITH FAITH GOD IS SO GOOD.

⤜⟩··⟨⤛

KNOWING THAT GOD IS WORKING WHERE
YOU CANNOT SEE HIM IS FAITH

Faithful Fridays

GOD MAKES A PROMISE,
FAITH BELIEVES IT,
HOPE ANTICIPATES IT,
AND
PATIENCE QUIETLY AWAITS IT.

Faithful Fridays

A COLLECTION OF FAITHFUL FRIDAY INSPIRATIONAL QUOTES

Who is Terri Avery?

Terri Avery is a Radio personality and program director, Inspirational speaker, Soul Coach, Author, Wife, Mom and Celebrator of Life!

I live my life by Hebrews 11:1
"Now, Faith is being sure of hope for and certain of what you do not see."

I was raised by a single mom, in The Bronx, NYC, along with my three brothers and life was not easy.

I believed in a dream, without knowing how it was going to happen. That dream was to get out of The Bronx and have a career in Radio. Success came, by the way of 25 plus years in the radio industry, countless radio industry awards, 3 beautiful daughters and a supportive husband. I now realized that a stronger power was controlling my life. The power of Faith!

I share my love for Fridays in this book with original quotes and pictures. The pictures are from places around the world that I loved visiting.

www.ingramcontent.com/pod-product-compliance
Lightning Source LLC
Chambersburg PA
CBHW040347060426
42445CB00029B/26